Conflict Resolution in the

Research on Teachers' Understanding and Implementing Conflict
Resolution Skills in the Early Childhood and Elementary Classroom

Samantha K. Jones-Woodard

Anew Beginning Educational Outreach, Inc.

ISBN-10: 1477509178
ISBN-13: 978-1477509173

Printed in the United States of America

Dedication

This book is dedicated in loving memory of my sister, Teresa S. Jones and in memory of my cousin and Godmother, Anna Mae White.

Preface

This book was designed as research primarily to explore school-based peer mediation and conflict resolution programs, and understand how early childhood and elementary teachers incorporated the collaborative problem-solving model into the student experience in the classroom. This research focused on how peer mediation and conflict resolution skills were used in the school, how and to what extent conflict resolution methods were integrated into the daily classroom activities, what factors accounted for teacher use or non-use of peer mediation/conflict resolution techniques in the classroom, and how teachers could be encouraged to use conflict resolution techniques in the classroom. This book can be used as a topic in staff development programs to help train teachers to integrate skills and concepts from the conflict resolution curriculum into the curricula that they teach. It may also help teachers to prepare a future plan of action that could reduce the number of recurring disciplinary problems so that they can concentrate on instructional content rather than classroom disputes.

The study involved a sample of 104 early childhood and elementary teachers in grades pre-kindergarten through grade 5. Questionnaires were used as the data source. While the study was limited by the number of teachers who participated in the survey, an analysis of the data showed that most teachers think providing students with conflict resolution skills is a positive benefit. The study also provided evidence that teachers are using some type of conflict resolution techniques. It was also concluded that when teachers did not teach conflict resolution skills more, it was mainly due to a lack of knowledge in the conflict resolution curriculum.

This book is not designed to be a conflict resolution program. It defines conflict resolution, gives the history of conflict resolution, and includes strategies, activities, and resources designed to address conflict resolution in the classroom. By implementing conflict resolution skills in the classroom, teachers can have a profound impact on students' behavior, as well as on the school climate.

Acknowledgements

First and foremost, I would like to thank God for helping me to achieve this accomplishment. Without Him, it would not have been possible. The honor, glory, and praise go to Him!

To my husband and best friend, Willie L. Woodard, Jr., who has sacrificed almost as much as myself during the completion of this book. He has without question provided me with love, patience, and support throughout the entire process of writing of this book. Thank you for having total confidence in everything that I do!

To my two sons, Dominique and Demetrius, thank you for your unconditional love, patience, support, willingness to help, and most of all, believing in Mommy. This has been a precious gift!

To my grandmother, Nora A.M. Jones, who instilled in me from an early age the value of hard work, excellence, a love for education and learning, and her enduring belief in my abilities. Her encouragement and support for my educational goals have made it all possible. Thanks Mother!

To my mom, Gwendolyn J. Shepard, during the difficult time of researching related literature. She contributed her time and effort in helping me to research related literature, which proved helpful and valuable. Thanks for helping me!

To my uncle, Walter Jones, Jr., for his support and interest during my research process. He has been a source of encouragement throughout the entire process. Thanks Uncle Walt!

To my cousin and Godsister, Herlena White Hagans, for her prayers, support, and encouragement. Thanks Sister!

To my friend, Tony B. Rogers, for his prayers, support, and computer knowledge during the final stages of this book. I am grateful to have him as a friend. Thanks Tony!

Finally, I would like to thank the superintendents and teachers of the school systems that allowed me the opportunity to use them for my surveys and data collection.

Table of Contents

Chapter   **Page**

Chapter 1

Introduction

Mediation and other conflict resolution techniques in schools today have become a national trend to reduce conflicts in the classrooms and overall school violence. As of 1995, over six thousand schools in the United States had begun school-based conflict resolution programs, and over three hundred students had been exposed to training in basic collaborative negotiation techniques (Girard & Koch, 1996). Many of these schools reported dramatic reductions in violence on the school campus discipline referrals, and drop out rates as a result of these programs. Conflict resolution programs are intuitively appealing to politicians and the public concerned about violence in schools as well as to participants in the community mediation movement (Rifkin, 1991). In the past, it has been difficult to find research data specifically addressing the effects of conflict resolution in elementary schools. It seemed as though a greater emphasis was placed on conflict resolution and peer mediation programs on middle and high school levels.

School-based conflict resolution and peer mediation programs have been known by many names: peer mediation, conflict resolution, student mediation, conflict management, and dispute resolution programs. Many programs strive to improve student self-esteem by allowing students to be responsible for solving their own conflicts and giving selected students a special role as peer mediators for the school. The two key components of school-based programs are (1) teaching conflict resolution in the classroom, and (2) training selected students to act as peer mediators (McKinney, Berdainsky, & Johnson, 1992).

School conflict resolution programs emerged from several sources: religious groups (Quakers, Mennonites), the peace movement, community mediation centers, the public health community, and the cooperative learning movement in education (Messing, 1991: Webster, 1991: Girard & Koch, 1996). Some programs emphasize identifying the destructive aspects of conflict and immediate crisis intervention techniques; others focus on the constructive aspects of conflict, by teaching long-term positive resolution methods such as negotiation and mediation (Raider, 1995). Most of the latter programs train all students in conflict resolution-negotiation skills and train selected students further in the mediation process (Johnson & Johnson, 1996). Children need models that demonstrate creative methods of managing conflict. There is very little research available about the role of adults in the school system in promoting the learning of conflict resolution in the classroom or of the transference of conflict resolution skills to conflict management in the classroom (Johnson, Johnson, & Dudley, 1992). Research regarding teachers' role is important because with adequate role models and opportunities to practice skills, students can make an attitude and behavior shift and assimilate appropriate conflict resolution choices into their repertoire of life skills (Gentry & Benenson, 1992; Johnson, Johnson, & Dudley, 1992). When teachers are committed to working with students as facilitators encouraging cooperative activities, and administrators are committed to developing a discipline system for the whole school that gives responsibility to students, teaching of conflict resolution skills is likely to be more effective (Tennent, 1996).

Peer mediation programs, where students are trained generally to resolve disputes involving other students, have been shown to be an effective means of resolving disputes in school settings. When given training, children successfully learn conflict resolution procedures to conflicts in and out of the classroom. There is anecdotal evidence that students transfer the mediation techniques learned in school settings beyond the classroom. Students have reported using their mediation skills to resolve disputes at home with their siblings and in their community with peers (Johnson, Johnson, & Dudley, 1992). By the time kindergartners are in the upper grades, they should be role models for the younger children in school. Many schools are implementing conflict resolution and peer mediation programs to reduce violence and student discipline problems in the school. The implementing of conflict resolution and peer mediation programs are preparing children how to learn to choose and use effective conflict resolution skills in their lives. These skills will not just benefit them at school, but also at home, in their neighborhoods, and in their future roles as citizens in society (Johnson, Johnson, & Dudley, 1992).

Statement of Problem

It is difficult to find research data specifically addressing the effects of conflict resolution in elementary schools. In the past, there was very little research available about the role of adults in the school system in promoting the learning of conflict resolution in the classroom or of the transference of conflict resolution skills to conflict management in the classroom (Johnson, Johnson, & Dudley, 1992). It seems as though a greater emphasis was placed on conflict resolution and peer mediation programs at middle and high school levels. The procedures necessary to manage conflict constructively are not established in most schools (DeCecco & Richards, 1974). Few teachers actually teach students the skills required for constructive conflict management. Without direct training in how to manage conflicts constructively, many students may never become able to do so (Johnson, Johnson, & Dudley, 1992). When students are learning new attitudes and behaviors, role modeling is very important (Kreidler, 1991).

For conflict resolution programs to be effective in schools, the adults in the school system need to feel personally comfortable using and modeling collaboration when dealing with problem-solving methods in the classroom setting (Conbere, 1994/1995). In order to better understand the role that teachers played in helping students develop conflict resolution skills, the focus was on understanding what part of the conflict resolution or peer mediation program was integrated into the school and how teachers incorporated the collaborative problem-solving strategies in the classroom.

Significance of Study

The objectives of the study were as follows:

1. To determine the role that early childhood and elementary teachers played in helping students develop conflict resolution skills.
2. To identify what methods early childhood and elementary teachers were using to teach conflict resolution skills in their classrooms.
3. To identify what methods early childhood and elementary teachers are using to teach conflict resolution skills in their classrooms.

4. To examine the attitudes of early childhood and elementary teachers toward the benefit of conflict resolution programs in the schools.

Methodology

The participants in the study were early childhood and elementary teachers from pre-kindergarten to grade 5. The study was conducted in 10 elementary schools (Pre-K- 5) in two counties. Teachers in these 10 elementary schools served as the research population. A questionnaire was developed to gather information to carry out research objectives. Appropriate approval from the county superintendents and principals was received to collect the data in their county and schools.

There were 10 pre-kindergarten teachers, 12 kindergarten teachers, 16 first grade teachers, 14 second grade teachers, 15 third grade teachers, 20 fourth grade teachers, and 17 fifth grade teachers. The teachers had varying years of teaching experiences ranging from 0-4 years to 30+ years.

A questionnaire was used to collect the required data for the study. The data was analyzed using sums and percentages. Ninety-nine percent of the teachers agreed that conflict resolution skills were important to teach children. It was interesting that approximately fifty-two percent of the teachers felt that teaching conflict resolution skills helped to reduce the number of students referred for disciplinary actions. Less than thirty-two percent of the teachers indicated that they did not incorporate conflict resolution skills in their classrooms because it was not needed. Roughly fifty-one percent of the teachers felt that their students were learning how to manage their conflicts constructively and to solve their own problems. Fifty-one percent of the teachers said that they did not incorporate conflict resolution skills in their classrooms because they lacked knowledge in the conflict resolution curriculum.

Limitations of Research

The study was limited by the number of teachers who participated in the survey. The survey only consisted of early childhood and elementary teachers (Pre-K- 5) in two counties with similar demographic characteristics. Another limitation was that teachers' actual responses may not have been their true feelings. As a result of these limitations, results may not apply to all school districts.

Definition of Terms

1. <u>Conflict Resolution Program</u>- A school-based program in which individuals learn and use collaborative communication and problem-solving skills and strategies such as negotiation and mediation, to resolve conflicts in a mutually peaceful and respectful way.

2. <u>Peer Mediation Program</u>- A component of the conflict resolution program where selected individuals are trained as mediators to handle conflicts that arise among peers.

3. <u>Negotiation</u>- A problem-solving process used by two individuals that are in conflict with each other. It involves agreeing to solve the problem, listening to each other, and brainstorming solutions that meet both people's needs.

4. <u>Mediation</u>- A process of communication and problem solving that leads to resolutions acceptable to all parties involved. The role of the mediator is to facilitate communication and problem solving between the parties and to help them find a win-win solution. This is a solution that satisfies both parties. The mediator helps the parties understand each other's concerns and assists in exploring options for resolving the conflict. The mediators are neutral helpers who do not take sides, act as judges, or give advice.

5. <u>Managing Conflict Constructively</u>- Handling conflicts in a helpful and productive way.

6. <u>Managing Conflicts Destructively</u>- Handling conflicts in a harmful and detrimental way.

7. <u>Incorporation of Conflict Resolution Skills into the Classroom</u>- Allowing students to use collaborative conflict resolution strategies (mediation and negotiation) in the classroom setting to settle interpersonal conflicts.

8. <u>Integration of Conflict Resolution Skills into the Curriculum</u>- An effort in which the teacher incorporates the concepts of conflict resolution into the material that is being taught in the classroom. Two examples are (1) using feeling words daily so that students can learn to identify and express different feelings and (2) having students to identify the different feelings of characters in stories and reading assignments, how they expressed their feelings, and how they might have chosen to express their feelings in a more appropriate way.

9. <u>Collaborative Problem Solving</u>- The use of problem solving based on the collaborative conflict resolution style in which all parties involved in conflict agree to discuss their interests and concerns and come to an agreement that meets the needs of each individual. This is also referred to as a win-win solution.

10. <u>Peaceable Classroom</u>- A safe and peaceable classroom is a classroom that involves improving the interpersonal relationships and conflict resolution skills of the students and teachers.

11. <u>Peaceable School</u>- A safe and peaceable school is a school that involves improving the interpersonal relationships and conflict resolution skills of the students, teachers, principals, parents, and the entire school staff.

12. <u>"I" messages</u>- Simple, powerful ways to communicate wants, needs, and feelings.

13. <u>Win-Win Resolution</u>- A conflict resolution process that aims to accommodate all disputants winning, in a way that all can profit from it in one way or the other.

14. <u>Disputant</u>- A person involved in an argument or a dispute.

15. <u>Dispute</u>- A disagreement, argument, debate, or controversy.

Chapter 2

Literature Review

Introduction

The purpose of this study was to explore reactions of teachers to school-based peer mediation and conflict resolution programs, and understand how they incorporated the collaborative problem-solving model into the students' experience in the classroom. Specifically, the study focused on how peer mediation and conflict resolution skills were used in the school, and how and to what extent conflict resolution methods were integrated into the daily classroom activities, what factors accounted for teacher use or non-use of peer mediation/conflict resolution techniques in the classroom, and how teachers could be encouraged to use conflict resolution techniques in the classroom. To provide a background for the study, a review of the literature focused on the following areas: (a) a history of school-based peer mediation and conflict resolution programs in the school, (b) the need for peer mediation and conflict resolution programs in the school, (c) the impact of peer mediation and conflict resolution programs on student behavior, (d) the impact of teacher classroom management and conflict resolution style in the classroom, and (e) the integration of conflict resolution programs into the school environment.

History of School-Based Mediation and Conflict Resolution Programs

The history of school-based mediation and conflict resolution programs may be traced to the 1960's, when teachers became active in non-violence training as part of the Civil Rights Movement (Cheatham, 1988). Throughout the 1960's and 1970's. religious and peace activists began to recognize the importance of teaching nonviolent means of conflict resolution to children. For example, many Quakers during this era became interested in applying the philosophy and skills of non-violence training to conflict resolution techniques for children. One of the first school mediation programs, Children's Creative Response to Conflict (CCRC) was created in 1972 and was originally sponsored by the Quaker Project on Community Conflict. This program focused attention changing the classroom atmosphere to one in which students felt secure and comfortable.

In the early 1980's, a national association called Educators for Social Responsibility (ESR) was formed, which was committed to promoting peace and socially conscious education (Cheatham, 1988). One member of this group, William Kreidler, published a conflict resolution curriculum that formed a basis for much of the work being carried out today. Working with the Boston Conflict Resolution Program, Kreidler stressed the importance of improving the classroom climate as a way to facilitate conflict resolution (Kreidler, 1991). The "Peaceable Classroom" had five qualities or themes: cooperation, communication, expression of feeling, appreciation of diversity, and conflict resolution. Kreidler worked with school systems across the country to start conflict resolution programs. According to Kreidler (1991): "This approach even helps children understand complex social and international conflicts. Teachers find that once students have a better understanding of conflict at the personal level, they are able to apply that understanding to larger conflicts. In effect, they are using conflict as an analogy to help them to think about larger adult conflicts. In the Boston Conflict Resolution Program, students have written letters to community and world leaders sharing their thoughts and ideas on handling major conflicts."

Another contribution to the development of mediation in the schools was made by the Carter Administration in the late 1970's when Neighborhood Justice Centers were introduced to communities around the country (Cheatham, 1988). One of the first of these centers to develop school mediation programs was the Community Board Program in San Francisco (Cheatham, 1988). Selected students were trained in mediation and then were available to mediate conflicts that erupted between students at the school. Since this first program, the Community Board has developed an extensive conflict resolution curriculum for students K-12, as well as a teaching guide and manuals for developing and implementing peer mediation programs. The curriculum includes lessons on awareness on different conflict resolution styles, understanding feelings, perceptions/diversity, active listening skills, "I" messages, and negotiation skills. Still widely used today, it was designed for use by classroom teachers as an ongoing course throughout the school year (Cheatham, 1988).

An important event for the future of school mediation took place in August 1984. The representatives of religious peace educators, community mediators, and the Educators of Social Responsibility came together to create the National Association for Mediation in Education (NAME) (Cheatham, 1988). NAME is housed at the Mediation Project of the University of Massachusetts in Amherst and has provided a network of support for conflict resolution programs in the schools with a bi-monthly newsletter, annual conferences, and regional networking activities. This organization is considered the primary national and international clearinghouse for information, resources, technical assistance, and training in the field of conflict resolution in education. They have helped to add mediation as an alternative to the traditional discipline procedures of suspension, detention, and expulsion (NAME, n.d.).

Over the past two decades, school mediation programs and conflict resolution curricula have been incorporated into schools across the United States as well as other countries including Canada, the United Kingdom, Australia, and New Zealand (Schacht, 1994). As of 1991, over 2,000 conflict resolution school programs were cited in the United States alone (Rifkin, 1991).

The Need for School-Based Peer Mediation and Conflict Resolution Programs

Recently school systems across the country have become concerned with the increased incidents of violence on the school campus. Violence in the schools was nominated as a primary public health concern in some states in 1992 (Schacht, 1994). For example, in 1992, the National Institute of Education reported that nearly 300,000 high school students were physically attacked each month, and one out of five students in grades nine through twelve carried a weapon. Recent FBI statistics show the number of murders, assaults, and weapon violations committed by youth aged 10 to 17 have more than doubled over the last 20 years (Statistical Abstract of the United States, 1994).

Creating a safe environment in the schools was critical for students to be able to learn. Extensive data illustrated that instances of violence, including bias-related violence and disciplinary problems in schools around the country, were severely interfering with the learning environment of students (Meek, 1992, 48). Studies have shown a correlation between a safe school environment and the ability of students to perform well academically (Mild, 1990). This study was significant in understanding what was needed for conflict resolution programs to positively impact the lives of students in elementary schools.

The rising incidence of violence in the schools has led numerous school districts to implement a wide range of costly safety measures from purchasing metal detectors to hiring full-time police officers. Although such measures may limit violent acts in the schools, they do not attack the causes of violence and often serve only to move the violence elsewhere in the community. There is a growing consensus that states the best way to handle violence in the schools and prevent its spread throughout the community is to defuse disputes before they turn violent (Trevaskis, 1994).

The increase in youth violence and its impact on schools underlies the importance of violence prevention efforts. Traditional efforts to reduce violence have been in a remedial capacity and often come too late after violent or maladaptive behaviors have become habitual (Cutrona & Guerin, 1994). However, children who have difficulty getting along with others tend to continue having problems throughout life indicating a need or early intervention. Because of the prevalence of violence in our society, a broad prevention response is needed in schools (Cutrona & Guerin, 1994).

The need for management of classroom disruptions was identified as one of the major concerns of education during the 1980s (Mild, 1990). Recently teachers have begun to voice concerns about coping with violence and increasing discipline problems in the classroom that keep them from being able to perform their teaching responsibilities. In a research paper presented at the Research Colloquia, "Issues in Education," Conn (1989) reported: "Being a classroom teacher for the past twenty years, I must say the ever increasing demands that a classroom teacher must meet in order to control conflict in the classroom and on the playground is sometimes overwhelming." "Over the years I have seen an ever increasing problem with violence and defiance of authority and social norms by the students in my school." (p.1)

The connection between conflict management and a child's developmental need was documented by Conn in 1989. Conn (1989) summarized developmental theory from several social scientists including Freud, Erickson, and Piaget and related it to conflict theory and developmental problems that occur in the classroom. Conn indicated that conflicts were a natural part of a child's developmental growth and that teachers needed to use conflict situations to help students learn.

Johnson, Johnson, and Dudley (1992) have shown that students learned how to solve problems in the classroom setting when exposed to mediation and negotiation training. Students developed constructive strategies for dealing with conflict and tended to feel empowered to solve problems themselves rather than turn to an adult for assistance. The study also showed that the numbers of conflicts in the classroom were reduced by 80% after students were trained in using appropriate conflict resolution techniques. These studies showed that when exposed to conflict resolution problem-solving models, students could not only keep conflict from interfering with the learning process, but they could also turn conflicts into learning experiences.

The Impact of Peer Mediation and Conflict Resolution Programs on Student Behavior

When conflict resolution programs were first implemented in public schools, the evaluative outcome data were very positive. Reports of reduction in discipline referrals, truancy, and suspension rates gave the programs national recognition (Lam, 1987). Anecdotal reports were even stronger. A high school student who participated in a mediation in New York City said: "All I ever wanted to do was fight. If someone said something to me I didn't like, I didn't think about talking; I just thought about fighting. I came into a mediation session as a disputant with four girls on the other side. I thought, Who needs this? What am I doing here? I just wanted to punch the girls out. I figured the mediator would tell me what I was going to have to do, but she didn't. Instead she drew me out, and listened to me. It felt so good to let it all out; then I wasn't angry anymore. I thought, Hey, if this can work for me, I want to learn how to do it." (Stuart 1991, p. 7)

Johnson, Johnson, and Dudley (1992) documented positive impacts of school-based conflict resolution programs. In a study to measure the conflict resolution training intervention in a fourth grade classroom, they verified that conflicts were prevalent in the classroom and showed that most students were involved with conflict on a daily basis. They study showed that students untrained in negotiation or mediation skills not only lacked knowledge in how to negotiate, but handled conflict by referring the dispute to the teacher, or using destructive strategies that tended to escalate the conflict. Students who participated in the intervention (negotiation and mediation training) were half as likely to ask the teacher to help with problems and never used destructive strategies to deal with conflicts. The authors recommended that all students in school receive negotiation and mediation training because this learning was not provided by families or the community. Their curriculum focused on teaching negotiation one-on-one and then using the mediation intervention when negotiation did not work.

In another study, Genty and Benenson (1992) showed that elementary students who were trained as peer mediators were able to transfer conflict resolution skills to the home setting with their siblings. After training, student mediators reported a significant decline in the frequency and intensity of conflict with their siblings. Over time, the parents of these children noted a significant improvement in the children's use of productive communication during conflicts and a significant decline in their own intervening actions. The authors indicated that teachers and principals requested peer mediation training for all students.

Teaching conflict resolution skills to youth may benefit future marriage and family relationships (Leckona, 1991). People who do not have the knowledge and skills to manage interpersonal conflict "are handicapped in their intimate relationships- marriage and parenting. If there is an absence of conflict resolution skills, this may lead to verbal or physical abuse" (Leckona, 1991).

Impact of Teacher Classroom Management and Conflict Resolution Style in the Classroom

The management of classroom conflict has been a national priority in schools across the United States (Mild, 1990). Few schools have measured the role that teachers play in helping students learn to deal with conflict in the classroom. In fact, experts have stated that too often teachers avoid conflict or try to suppress conflict in the classroom, and that teachers "need to be able to channel controversy, and use it as an opportunity for learning" (Kreidler, 1991). In a study of the use of negotiation and mediation in the classroom, researchers recommend that "classrooms need to become places where destructive conflicts are prevented and where constructive conflicts are structured, encouraged, and utilized to improve the quality of instruction and classroom life" (Johnson, Johnson, & Dudley, 1992).

Studies have shown that the teacher plays a critical role in establishing the learning environment of the classroom (Mild, 1990). The teacher must be sensitive to the content as well as the development of self when structuring and delivering the learning. According to Mild, "Since institutionalized education is a communication process in which the instructor largely controls and assumes responsibility for student learning, the importance of communication in defining a teaching style that promotes a healthy learning environment cannot be understated" (p.4).

Joyce, Weil, and Showers (1992) provided an in-depth description of different teaching styles as they affected the student learning experience. They categorized an array of teaching models into four families based on educational philosophy and processes. One, the social family group, focused on developing cooperative relationships in the classroom to take advantage of collective group energy. The teacher played the role of facilitator and academic counselor and provided learning activities in small groups to enhance the creative interaction of the learning process. One example of the social family group, cooperative learning, was recently the focus of intensive research and development. The second model, information processing, was based on enhancing the individual's "innate drive to make sense of the world by acquiring and organizing data" (p.7). Teaching models in this group focused on helping students learn how to think effectively by learning information, concepts, and developing the ability to analyze information. The third group, defined as the personal family, focused on helping students to understand themselves better and take responsibility for their education. One model, nondirective teaching, was based on Carl Rogers' theories of teaching which are oriented around the student's perceptual world. In this model the teacher facilitated the learning process by determining the students' needs and helping to design activities that met those needs. The fourth group was defined as the behavior systems family and was founded on the work of B.F. Skinner. This group included models such as behavior modification, behavior therapy, and cybernetics. It was based on the philosophy that "human beings are self-correcting communication systems that modify behavior in response to information" (p. 10). The teacher structured the social system of the classroom by selecting materials or processes, which directed the learning through rewards and punishments. Inappropriate behavior was ignored, or when necessary, isolation (time out) was used to restructure behavior.

In each of these models, the teacher played a key role in managing students' behavior as part of the learning process. The social and personal family groups focused on student-directed activities and required the use of negotiation and collaborative problem- solving to resolve conflict. In these models, students learning how to mange and resolve conflicts as part of the total learning process. The informational and behavioral models focused on the teacher as the director of the learning process. In these models, the focus was on individual mastery of content. Conformity of behavior was considered important for the maximum learning of the whole group. In these models, teachers handled student conflict themselves since they perceived that conflict would interfere with the learning process.

Studies have shown that discipline strategies used by teachers in the classroom affect students' self-development. In a recent study on teacher style, Burton (1993) found that many times teachers were unaware that their choice of discipline strategy negated their purpose of changing student behavior. Burton found that teachers most often chose discipline strategies they felt would provide for personal growth of the students. In many cases, however, she found that the techniques used to support these strategies contradicted the teacher's purpose. When teachers used punishment to discipline aggressive students, they indicated that they intended this as part of a self-control strategy for long-term change. Burton suggested that teachers needed to be aware of the negative impact some of their discipline choices had on the self-development of students.

Mild (1990) also studied teacher styles in the classroom and measured students' reactions to several different conflict resolution styles by teachers. He found that students in third through eighth grades preferred teachers to use collaborative, problem-solving approach for student conflicts. Students preferred to have an opportunity to participate directly in finding resolutions to conflicts.

Johnson (1991) found that teachers who attended 30-hour conflict resolution course changed their strategies for dealing with conflicts with both peers and students. After the course, teachers increased their use of dominating style with students and peers. They reported that the course had enhanced their effectiveness in managing conflict in the school setting. With practice, conflict resolution will come naturally to children, as well as teachers. Teachers must ask meaningful questions that allow children to solve their own problems during this process (Koplow, 2002).

The Integration of Conflict Resolution into the School Environment

Conflict resolution skills should be a fundamental part of the school's curriculum, discipline strategies, and management style. It is important that collaborative decision-making be adopted by all members of the school team. Studies have shown that the conflict resolution style chosen by administrators impacts the total school environment. In one study, teachers were surveyed on their perceptions of the relationship of the school principal's conflict management behavior to the overall school climate. Hoover (1990) found that principals who were perceived as more frequently using problem solving, accommodation, and compromising styles were associated with schools that had lower conflict levels. Principals who were perceived to rely on forcing and avoiding behavior in conflict situations, on the other hand, administered high conflict levels.

In an article entitled "Peer Mediation in a Context of Systemic Change" Conbere (1994/1995) discussed the problems inherent in changing the school environment. He stated: "Even when students are taught these skills and are given the opportunity to test out and internalize them in mediation, they may not take root. The factors that undercut the teaching of conflict resolution are factors connected to systemic change. Adding a peer mediation program and teaching conflict resolution may have little effect if the school itself does not undergo some significant changes." (p. 5)

Conbere (1994/1995) indicated that school-based changes involved time, curricula, discipline, staff interactions with parents, staff interactions with each other, space, finances, and staff development. Specifically, problems arose when staff were expected to work collaboratively but were not trained how to do it. "Therefore if staff conflict is ongoing, and if the source is stress from an attempt to implement shared decision-making in the school, then this part of school as system may have to be resolved before staff can have the energy to undertake the changes that are part of starting a mediation program. A more difficult issue for staff is that if they cannot resolve their own conflicts, they cannot adequately teach students to do otherwise. We all learn more from actions than from words. Staff who do not really believe they can safely resolve conflict because they do not experience this with their peers; will have a difficult time encouraging students to try." (Conbere, p. 11).

It appears that integration of conflict resolution into schools and classrooms required an attitude change about resolving conflict collaboratively by all individuals in the school –the students, the teachers, and the administrators. As change is generally resisted, the administrator needed to model collaboration through support and leadership. In addition, a commitment to use collaboration decision-making in all aspects of the school environment was critical for these programs to succeed.

Lantieri (2003) reported that comprehensive violence-prevention programs, such as the Resolving Conflict Creatively Program (RCCP), teach effective communication and peaceful conflict resolution to teachers, children, parents, and school administration and staff. Using this program in a school for only one year showed some encouraging results: "92% of children felt better about themselves; and more than 90% of parents reported an increase in their own communication and problem-solving skills.

Chapter Summary

Conflict resolution and peer mediation programs have developed over the years in response to the growing concern of violence in society and the increasing incidences of violence in the schools. Creating a safe environment in the schools is critical for students to be able to learn. Studies have shown a correlation between a safe school environment and the ability of students to perform well academically.

The increase in youth violence and its impact on schools contributed to the need of school-based mediation and conflict resolution programs. Research has shown that students learned how to solve problems in the classroom setting when exposed to mediation and negotiation training. In addition, students exposed to intensive training in collaborative problem-solving strategies (mediation and negotiation) not only become proficient in solving conflicts, but also perceived that dealing with conflict can result in personal learning. Thus, they change their attitude that conflict is "negative" and become empowered to view conflict as a problem-solving challenge. Over the past decades, school mediation programs and conflict resolution programs have been incorporated into the schools across the United States as well as other countries including Canada, the United Kingdom, Australia, and New Zealand.

Studies have shown that teachers played an important role in the use of collaborative problem-solving strategies in the classroom. They have also shown that discipline strategies used by teachers in the classroom affect student's self development. When exposed to intensive training in conflict resolution strategies, teachers tended to improve their ability to deal with conflicts both among their peers and with their students. In order for peer mediation and conflict resolution programs to be effective, all segments of the school population needed to be committed.

Past research has focused on exploring student behavior towards conflict resolution as well as the impact of teacher and administrator attitudes on the overall school environment. These studies have not explored why teachers resist accepting and integrating peer mediation and conflict resolution strategies in the classroom environment. This research focused on gathering information on the factors that contributed to why teachers were using or not using conflict resolution skills in the classroom. It explored how teachers incorporated the collaborative problem-solving model in the student experience.

Chapter 3

Methodology

Introduction

The purpose of this study was to explore teachers' attitudes and their use of conflict resolution skills in the classroom.

Population

Two school systems were chosen to conduct the study. These school systems had both experienced two disasters, which appeared to have some impact on the behavior of students. These two disasters, one after the other, made an enormous impact. Many students and their families evacuated to shelters for months. Others had to live with multiple families or relocate to another area. These students had to endure the loss of loved ones, homes, clothes, material objects, pets, and economical losses. Many of their parents and guardians loss jobs due to businesses being destroyed. Schools systems were closed for days. After students returned to school, they were faced with obstacles dealing with class work and their loss. This appeared to have some impact on the behavior of students.

To respect the privacy of these two school systems, they will be referred to as School System A and School System B. School System A had a population of around 19,000 people and School System B had a population of around 60,000.

Description of Sample

The participants in the study were 104 early childhood and elementary teachers in pre-kindergarten through grade 5. There were 10 pre-kindergarten teachers, 12 kindergarten teachers, 16 first grade teachers, 14 second grade teachers, 15 third grade teachers, 20 fourth grade teachers, and 17 fifth grade teachers. There were 51 teachers from School System A and 53 teachers from School System B.

The teachers had varying years of teaching experiences ranging from 0-4 years to 30+ years. 19.2 percent had 0-4 years, 17.3 percent had 5-9 years, 15.4 percent had 10-14 years, 12.5 percent had 15-19 years, 13.5 percent had 20-24 years, 13.5 percent had 25-29 years, and 8.7 percent had 30+ years.

Description of Instrument

There was not a particular one instrument found that was already available that would be appropriate. Based upon the instruments found, knowledge was received from them to develop the instrument for the study. A research questionnaire was developed to gather the data to answer the research objectives. The questionnaire was pilot tested on teachers in a class at a major university. Based upon feedback and remarks, the final questionnaire was developed and printed for use.

Procedure

Once permission was received from superintendents and principals, 200 plus packages were prepared with the instruments and instructions on completing the instruments. The approximate number of Pre-K- 5 teachers in each school in the two counties was gathered. Packages for the approximate number of teachers were delivered to each school and a collection box was placed in the counselor's office for the teachers to place the instruments once they were completed. Various amounts of time were spent at each school in effort to establish rapport with the counselor and the teachers.

A date was given as to when the boxes would be picked up from the schools. The instructions in the package asked teachers to complete them within five days after receiving them but preferably as soon as possible once they received them.

Once the deadline for picking up the boxes came, there was a visit to each school to receive the boxes. The instruments did not require any names or identification. Once the questionnaires were collected, the data was coded and inputted into the SPSS Program to be analyzed. The data was analyzed using descriptive statistics and charts.

Chapter 4

Presentation and Analysis of Data

This chapter presents the data analyzed and a discussion of the results. The main purpose of the study was to explore early childhood and elementary teachers' attitudes toward conflict resolution and to determine the use of conflict resolution skills in their classrooms. To accomplish this purpose, there were four main objectives for the study.

The objectives for the study were as follows:
1. To determine the role that early childhood and elementary teachers played in helping students develop conflict resolution skills.
2. To identify what methods early childhood and elementary teachers were using to teach conflict resolution skills in their classrooms.
3. To examine the attitudes of early childhood and elementary teachers toward the benefit of conflict resolution programs in the schools.

One hundred four teachers returned usable questionnaires, which were used for the data in the study. Twenty (19.2%) of the teachers had 0-4 years of teaching experience; eighteen (17.3%) of the teachers had 5-9 years of teaching experience; sixteen (15.4%) of the teachers had 10-14 years of teaching experience; thirteen (12.5%) of the teachers had 15-19 years of teaching experience; fourteen (13.5%) of the teachers had 20-24 years of teaching experience; fourteen (13.5%) of the teachers had 25-29 years of teaching experience; nine (8.7%) of the teachers had 30 or more years of teaching experience.

All of the one hundred four teachers taught pre-kindergarten through grade 5. Ten (9.6%) of the teachers taught pre-kindergarten; twelve (11.5%) of the teachers taught kindergarten; twenty (19.2%) of the teachers taught fourth grade; seventeen (16.3%) of the teachers taught fifth grade; sixteen (15.4%) of the teachers taught first grade; fifteen (14.4%) of the teachers taught third grade; fourteen (13.5%) of the teachers taught second grade.

The first set of eight questions dealt with how teachers described their feelings toward certain statements related to conflict resolution. Even though the responses were collected on a five-point scale, the results were collapsed into three categories for more clarification. Response number one made up the first category, which remained the same "Never." Responses two and three made up the second category and were called "Sometimes." Responses four and five made up the third category and were called "Frequently."

For question one "I teach conflict resolution skills in my classroom on a daily basis" thirty teachers (28.8%) checked never; fifty-five teachers (52.9%) checked sometimes; and nineteen teachers (18.3%) checked frequently. For question two "I use role-playing to teach conflict resolution skills in the classroom," forty-two teachers (40.4%) checked never; fifty-three teachers (50.9%) checked sometimes; and nine teachers (8.7%) checked frequently. For question three "I use puppetry to teach conflict resolution skills in the classroom," sixty-six teachers (63.5%) checked never; thirty-six (34.6%) checked sometimes; and two (1.9%) checked frequently. For question four "I use other techniques to teach conflict resolution skills in the classroom," thirty-five teachers (33.7%) checked never; fifty-two (50%) checked sometimes; and seventeen (16.3%) checked frequently.

When the question "I change the way that I organize my class to include skill building in conflict resolution" was answered, twenty-five teachers (24.0%) checked never; sixty-nine (66.4%) checked sometimes; and ten (9.6%) checked frequently. Continuing with question six "I integrate skills and concepts from the conflict resolution curriculum into the curricula that I teach," twenty-four teachers (23.1%) checked never; sixty-six (63.5%) checked sometimes; and fourteen (13.4%) checked frequently. For question number seven "I give students who exhibit appropriate behavior a special role as peer mediators in my classroom," forty-five teachers (43.3%) checked never; thirty-two (30.8%) checked sometimes; and twenty-seven (25.9%) checked frequently. For the eighth and final question in this category " I encourage cooperative activities in my classroom" ten teachers (9.6%) checked never; sixty-four (61.5%) checked sometimes; and thirty (28.9%) checked frequently. (See Appendix for Table 1 and Results.)

The second set of questions dealt with how teachers described their feelings toward conflict resolution. Again, the responses were collapsed from a five-point scale to three categories. Responses one and two made up the first category and were called "Agree." Response three remained the same and made up the second category "Not sure." Responses four and five made up the third category and were called "Disagree."

For question one in the second set of eight questions "I feel that conflict resolution skills are important to teach children," one hundred three teachers (99.0%) checked agree; one (1%) checked not sure; and no one checked disagree. For the second question "By teaching conflict resolution skills in the classroom, fewer students have been referred for disciplinary actions" forty-three teachers (41.4%) checked agree; fifty-four (51.9%) checked not sure; and seven (6.7%) checked disagree. For question three "My students are learning how to manage their own conflicts constructively and to solve their own problems" fifty-three teachers (50.9%) checked agree; thirty-nine (37.6%) checked not sure; and twelve (11.5%) checked disagree. For question four "I do not incorporate conflict resolution skills in my classroom because teaching conflict resolution requires too much time" sixty-nine teachers (66.3%) checked agree; two teachers (1.9%) checked not sure; and thirty-three teachers (31.8%) checked disagree.

Continuing with the second set of eight questions, question five stated "I do not incorporate conflict resolution skills in my classroom due to a lack of knowledge in the conflict resolution curriculum' forty-two teachers (41.3%) checked agree; five teachers (4.8%) checked not sure; and forty-six teachers (53.9%) checked disagree. For question six, " I do not incorporate conflict resolution skills in my classroom because it is not required at my school" fifty-three teachers (51.0%) checked agree; nine teachers (8.6%) checked not sure; and forty-two teachers (40.4%) checked disagree. For question seven " I do not incorporate conflict resolution skills in my classroom because it is not needed" fifteen teachers (14.4%) checked agree; four teachers (3.8%) checked not sure; and eighty-five teachers (81.8%) checked disagree. For the final question eight "I know some schools that are getting good results by requiring teachers to incorporate conflict resolution skills in the classroom" fifty-one teachers (49.0%) checked agree; forty teachers (38.5%) checked not sure; and thirteen teachers (12.5%) checked disagree. (See Appendix for Table 2 and for Results.)

Chapter 5

Discussion of Results, Conclusions, and Recommendations

The main purpose of this book was designed as research primarily to explore early childhood and elementary teachers' attitudes toward conflict resolution and their use of conflict resolution in the classroom. One hundred four teachers from ten schools in two joining counties provided the data for the research. More than eighty percent of the teachers had more than four years of teaching experience. All of the one hundred four teachers were teaching grades pre-kindergarten through grade five.

A questionnaire was developed and used to collect the required data for the study. The data was analyzed using sums and percentages. When the first set of questions were analyzed which dealt with how teachers described their feelings toward certain statements related to conflict resolution, the findings were of interest. More than sixty-three percent of the participating teachers indicated that they have never used puppetry to teach conflict resolution skills in the classroom. Approximately seventy percent of the teachers indicated that they frequently used role-playing to teach conflict resolution skills in the classroom. Only roughly ten percent of the teachers indicated that they have never used cooperative activities in their classrooms. Approximately sixty-six percent of the teachers used some techniques to teach conflict resolution skills in their classrooms.

The second set of eight questions were concerned with how teachers felt about conflict resolution and its use. Ninety-nine percent of the teachers agreed that conflict resolution skills were important to teach children. It was interesting that approximately fifty-two percent of the teachers felt that teaching conflict resolution skills helped to reduce the number of students referred for disciplinary actions. Less than thirty-two percent of the teachers indicated that they did not incorporate conflict resolution skills in their classrooms because it was not needed. Roughly fifty-one percent of the teachers felt that their students were learning how to manage their conflicts constructively and to solve their own problems. Fifty-one percent of the teachers said that they did not incorporate conflict resolution skills in their classrooms because they lacked knowledge in the conflict resolution curriculum.

It was concluded from the study that most teachers think providing students with conflict resolution skills is a positive benefit. The study also provided evidence that teachers are using some type or types of conflict resolution techniques. It was also concluded that when teachers did not teach conflict resolution skills more, it was mainly due to a lack of knowledge in the conflict resolution curriculum.

As a result of reviewing the literature for this study and the results of this study, the following recommendations are offered:

1. It is recommended that teachers be provided more training through workshops and seminars on conflict resolution skills.
2. It is recommended that conflict resolution skills be taught in the classroom to students when appropriate.
3. It is recommended that additional research be conducted for other grade levels to determine conflict resolution use and benefits.

Appendix

A Few Strategies for Implementing Conflict Resolution Skills in the Classroom

1. Discuss conflict resolution and positive ways to resolve conflicts.

2. Increase children's ability to read nonverbal cues.

3. Help children see that others may have a different view.

4. Provide many opportunities for trial and error.

5. Encourage children to draft a conflict plan.

6. Provide many ways for children to feel successful.

7. Support children's self-esteem through meaningful activities.

8. Help children to find more effective ways of behaving toward friends.

9. Model good social skills.

10. Discuss characteristics that foster friendship.

11. Praise children for successful interactions.

12. Discuss words that describe feelings and emotions.

A Few Activities for Implementing Conflict Resolution Skills in the Classroom

1. Have role-playing activities on resolving conflicts.

2. Have puppet shows and finger plays on resolving conflicts.

3. Read stories on handling conflicts.

4. Read stories on social skills, and friendships.

5. Recite poems on handling conflicts.

6. Recite poems on social skills and friendships.

7. Have cultural scenes to learn about different cultures.

8. Use picture problems to identify the right way to resolve conflicts.

9. Play games on learning how to be fair.

10. Identify and define words that relate to feelings and emotions.

11. Making greeting cards using words that express feelings and emotions.

12. Play "getting to know me" games for students to learn about themselves.

13. Play "getting to know you" games for students to learn about others.

14. Do journal writing on "Being True Friends" (For younger students, picture journals may be substituted.)

15. Make a conflict web with the word "conflict" being in the center and then discuss things that can cause conflicts.

16. Make a book showing the conflict resolution steps to solving a problem.

17. Do a conflict resolution word search with words generated from the computer program Puzzle Maker.

18. Do a conflict resolution crossword puzzle with words generated on the computer using Crossword Magic.

19. Make a conflict resolution chart for vocabulary words.

20. Make a family collage by having students cut different pictures from magazines. Encourage students to cut different types of families (multiple parents, single parent, interracial, extended, etc.)

21. Play a game of Silhouettes and have students to copy one another. Discuss how it feels to be copied.

22. Have a whole group discussion on the following sayings:

    (a) One rotten apple spoils the bunch.

    (b) He is a bad apple.

    (c) She is the apple of my eye.

Poem

(Poem Written by Samantha Jones-Woodard)

True Friendship

True friendship is like a circle,
the bond never ends.
We may have our conflicts,
but with conflict resolution, it always mends.
Without conflict resolution,
our friendship may be broken.
Then we may become enemies,
with words unspoken.
Conflict resolution is the name of the game.
Without it, things will never be the same.
Our circle of friendship is genuine and true.
A true friend is what I have found in you.

From *Conflict Resolution in the Classroom: Research on Teachers' Understanding and Implementing Conflict Resolution Skills in the Early Childhood and Elementary Classroom* by Samantha Jones-Woodard, copyright © 2012

Poem

(Poem Written by Samantha Jones-Woodard)

I Am Special

When I look into the mirror
this is what I see;
A very special person,
and that would be me.
I am unique in my very own way.
I may not be perfect,
but that's okay.
I may not be like all of the rest,
but I strive to be my very best.
I am special!

From *Conflict Resolution in the Classroom: Research on Teachers' Understanding and Implementing Conflict Resolution Skills in the Early Childhood and Elementary Classroom* by Samantha Jones-Woodard, copyright © 2012

Poem

(Poem Written by Samantha Jones-Woodard)

Conflict Resolution

Conflict resolution results in a positive solution.
We have a voice to make a better choice.
If we have little respect,
then it will cause a ripple effect.
We have to keep in sight
and do what is right.
When we get along,
our friendships stay strong.
Conflict Resolution!

From *Conflict Resolution in the Classroom: Research on Teachers' Understanding and Implementing Conflict Resolution Skills in the Early Childhood and Elementary Classroom* by Samantha Jones-Woodard, copyright © 2012

Poem

(Poem Written by Samantha Jones-Woodard)

Friendship Apple Sale

I have apples for you and me.

They are red as you can see.

If you put them in the pail,

Then we can have an apple sale.

From *Conflict Resolution in the Classroom: Research on Teachers' Understanding and Implementing Conflict Resolution Skills in the Early Childhood and Elementary Classroom* by Samantha Jones-Woodard, copyright © 2012

Resources

Books

All I Really Need to Know I Learned in Kindergarten by Robert Fulghum (Boston: G.K. Hall, 1988). This book emphasizes respect, sharing, playing fair, not hitting people, and saying that you are sorry when you hurt someone. For all ages.

Bailey the Big Bully by Lizi Boyd (New York: Viking Kestrel, 1989). All of the kids are afraid of Bailey, the bully. Bailey is big, mean, and always gets his way. The only one that is not afraid is Max, the new boy in town. For grades K-3.

Dear God, Help! Love, Earl by Barbara Park (New York: Knopf, 1993). Eddie Wilber and his friends are tired of being bullied and having to pay protection money to the school bully, Eddie McPhee. Eddie Wilber and his friends, Maxie and Rosie come up with a scheme to seek revenge. For grades 3-5.

First Grade King by Karen L. Williams (New York: Clarion Books, 1992). First-grader Joey King experiences making friends, learning to read, and dealing with the class bully. For grades K-3.

Good Friends are Hard to Find by Fred Frankel (Glendale, CA: Perspective Publishing, 1996). This book has step-by-step ideas to help children make friends and solve problems with other kids. For grades K-6.

How to Lose All Your Friends by Nancy Carlson (New York: Viking Penguin, 1994). Carlson makes fun at bullies, grumps, whiners, poor sports, and other kids who alienate others. For grades K-3.

I Like Me! by Nancy L. Carlson (New York: Viking, 1988). A charming pig proves the best friend that you can have is yourself. For grades preschool- 3.

Push & Shove by Jim and Joan Boulden (Weaverville, CA: Boulden Publishing, 1994). The reader will discover how both the bully and the victim feel. For grades 2-4.

The Rat and the Tiger by Kelko Kasza (New York: G.P. Putnam, 1993). In Rat and Tiger's friendship, Rat has to stand up for himself. For grades K-3.

Why is Everybody Always Picking on Me: A Guide to Handling Bullies by Terrence Webster-Doyle (Middlebury, VT: Atrium Society, 1991). Stories and activities on how to resolve conflicts nonviolently. For grades K-5.

Videos

Bully Breath: How to Tame a Troublemaker (19 minutes). In this video, real-life situations are dramatized and then discussed, helping to understand the reasons behind a bully's behavior as well as specific steps to neutralize their power. For elementary students. Available from The National Center for Violence Prevention, PO Box 9, 102 Highway 81 North, Calhoun, KY 42327.

Conflict! Think About It, Talk About It, Try to Work It Out (15 minutes). In this video, two children use the game called "Anger Commander" when they find out that sometimes handling their anger approximately is not enough to avoid conflicts with others.

Dealing with Anger plus Cool, Calm and Collected (two videos), 33 minutes total). This video teaches students to learn to identify the sources of their anger, where is comes from, and what situations are most likely to cause it. Included with these videos is a teacher's guide with lesson plans, student activities, and discussion questions. For grades 4-6. Available from The National Center for Violence Prevention, PO Box 9, 102 Highway 81 North, Calhoun, KY 42327.

Don't Pick on Me! (20 minutes). This video examines the dynamics behind teasing and models effective responses to being harassed. A teacher's guide is included. For grades 3-8. Available from the National Center for Violence Prevention, PO Box 9, 102 Highway 81 North, Calhoun, KY 42327.

Keeping Cool: Anger Management Tools (60 minutes). This video teaches techniques of anger control, conflict resolution, effective communication, and problem solving. For all ages. Available from The National Center for Violence Prevention, PO Box 9, 102 Highway 81 North, Calhoun, KY 42327.

Peace on the Playground (27 minutes). This video teaches children and parents how to deal with violence and the dangers of guns. For elementary and middle school students. Available from Films for Humanities & Science, PO Box 2053, Princeton, NJ 08543.

Resolving Conflicts (28 minutes). Tuggy and Rhonda learn that there are ways to resolve disagreement without fighting. They learn to work out interpersonal conflicts in a peaceful and positive way. For grades 2-4. Available from The National Center for Violence Prevention, PO Box 9, 102 Highway 81 North, Calhoun, KY 42327.

Tug of War: Strategies for Conflict Resolution (25 minutes). Portrayal of children's anger and illustrations of different ways of handling conflict without adult supervision is the lesson of this video. For all ages. Available from The National Center for Violence Prevention, PO Box 9, 102 Highway 81 North, Calhoun, KY 42327.

Organizations

Center for Prevention of School Violence
20 Enterprise Street, Suite 2
Raleigh, NC 27607
Telephone: (800) 299-6054
http://www.ncsu.edu/cpsv/

The Center for Prevention of School Violence focuses on ensuring that schools are safe and secure by creating an atmosphere that is conducive to learning.

Children's Creative Response to Conflict (CCRC)
PO Box 271
523 North Broadway
Nyack, NY 10960-0271
Telephone: (914) 353-1796

Children's Creative Response to Conflict (CCRC) provides conflict resolution training based on peer leadership to children, adolescents, teachers, and parents. It emphasizes problem solving, mediation, cooperation, and communication.

The National Association for Mediation in Education
205 Hampshire House
Box 33635
Amherst, MA 01003
Telephone: (413) 545-2462

The National Association for Mediation in Education produces a newsletter called *The Fourth R.*

National School Safety Center (NSSC)
141 Duesenberg Drive, Suite 11
Westlake Village, CA 91362
Telephone: (805) 373-9977
http://nssc1.org/

The National School Safety Center (NSSC) offers booklets on conflict resolution, bullying, and violence prevention for educators and parents.

Peacebuilders
c/o Heartsprings, Inc.
PO Box 12158
Tucson, AZ 85732
Telephone: (520) 322-9977
Fax: (520) 322-9983
http://peacebuilders.com

Psychologist Dennis Embry created Peacebuilders. It is a community-based program designed to help create a school environment that reduces violence. The program focuses on four basic principles: praise people, give up put-downs, notice hurts and right the wrongs, and seek wise people.

Resolving Conflict Creatively Program (RCCP)
40 Exchange Place, Suite 1111
New York, NY 10005
Telephone: (212) 509-0022
Fax: (212) 509-1095

Resolving Conflict Creatively Program (RCCP) is an initiative of Educators for Social Responsibility. It is a school-based program conflict resolution program that provides a model for preventing violence and creating caring learning communities.

Teaching Tolerance
400 Washington Avenue
Montgomery, AL 36104
Telephone: (334) 264-0286
http://www.splcenter.org/teachingtolerance/tt-index.html

Teaching Tolerance is a national education project that helps teachers foster equity, respect, and understanding in the classroom.

Websites

Bullies: A Serious Problem for Kids
National Crime Prevention Prevention Council (NCPC)
http://www.ncpc.org/10adu3.htm

This website provides tips to teachers and parents about what they can do to help prevent bullying.

Family Education Network
http://create.familyeducation.com/

This website has articles, a message board, and advice from experts on keeping children safe in school. Search using the phrase "Back to School Safety."

Kidscape
http://www.kidscape.org.uk/kidscape/

This website is about keeping children safe. The information focuses on preventing bullying before it happens.

CONFLICT RESOLUTION QUESTIONNAIRE

DIRECTIONS: Please check (X) one of the following that indicates the years of experience that you have as a teacher.

(___) 0-4 years

(___) 5-9 years

(___) 10-14 years

(___) 20-24 years

(___) 25-29 years

(___) 30+ years

What grade do you teach?

(___) Pre-Kindergarten

(___) Kindergarten

(___) First

(___) Second

(___) Third

(___) Fourth

(___) Fifth

This is a questionnaire to find out your experiences and opinions on integrating conflict resolution skills in the classroom. It is divided into 2 sections, each consisting of 8 statements concerning conflict resolution. There are no right or wrong answers. On the next 2 pages, read each statement carefully and circle one number for each line that best describes your feelings based on the following scales:

SECTION 1.

Never
Rarely
Sometimes
Frequently
Always

SECTION 2.

Strongly Agree
Agree
Not Sure
Strongly Disagree
Disagree

Section 1.

Read each statement carefully and circle one number for each line that best describes your feelings from the following scale: (1) Never (2) Rarely (3) Sometimes (4) Frequently (5) Always.

Statements	Never	Rarely	Sometimes	Frequently	Always
I teach conflict resolution in my classroom on a daily basis.	1	2	3	4	5
I use role-playing to teach conflict resolution skills in the classroom.	1	2	3	4	5
I use puppetry to teach conflict resolution skills in the classroom.	1	2	3	4	5
I use other techniques to teach conflict resolution skills in the classroom.	1	2	3	4	5

I change the way I organize my class and daily routine to include skill building in conflict resolution.	1	2	3	4	5
I integrate skills and concepts from the conflict resolution curriculum into the curricula that I teach.	1	2	3	4	5
I give students who exhibit appropriate behavior a special role as peer mediators in my classroom.	1	2	3	4	5
I encourage cooperative activities in my classroom.	1	2	3	4	5

Section 2.

Read each statement carefully and circle one number for each line that best describes your feelings from the following scale: (1) Strongly Agree (2) Agree (3) Not Sure (4) Strongly Disagree (5) Disagree.

My students are learning how to manage their conflicts constructively and to solve their own problems.	1	2	3	4	5
I do not incorporate conflict resolution skills in my classroom because teaching conflict resolution requires too much time.	1	2	3	4	5
I do not incorporate conflict resolution skills in my classroom due to a lack of knowledge in the conflict resolution curriculum.	1	2	3	4	5
I do not incorporate conflict resolution skills in my classroom because it is not required at my school.	1	2	3	4	5
I do not incorporate conflict resolution skills in my classroom because it is not needed.	1	2	3	4	5
I know some schools that are getting good results by requiring teachers to incorporate conflict resolution skills in the classroom.	1	2	3	4	5

Table 1.

Statements	Never	Percent Never	Sometimes	Percent Sometimes	Frequently	Percent Frequently
I teach conflict resolution in my classroom on a daily basis.	30	28.8	55	52.9	19	18.3
I use role-playing to teach conflict resolution skills in the classroom.	42	40.4	53	50.9	9	8.7
I use puppetry to teach conflict resolution skills in the classroom.	66	63.5	36	34.6	2	1.9
I use other techniques to teach conflict resolution skills in the classroom.	35	33.7	52	50	17	16.3
I change the way I organize my class and daily routine to include skill building in conflict resolution.	25	24	69	66.4	10	9.6
I integrate skills and concepts from the conflict resolution curriculum into the curricula that I teach.	24	23.1	66	63.5	14	13.4
I give students who exhibit appropriate behavior a special role as peer mediators in my classroom.	45	43.3	32	30.8	27	25.9
I encourage cooperative activities in my classroom.	10	9.6	64	61.5	30	28.9

Chart 1.

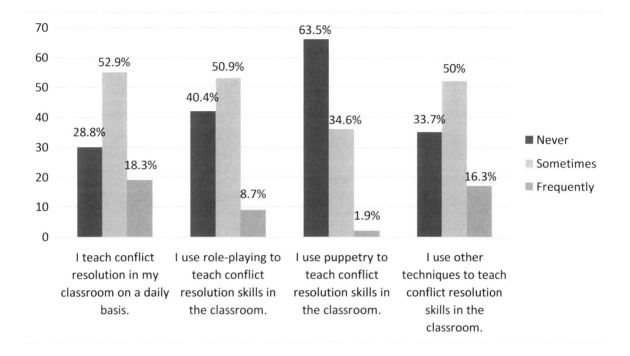

Chart 1. (continued)

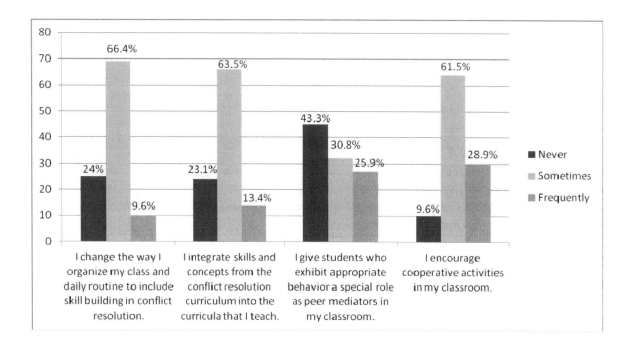

Table 2A.

Statements	Agree	Percent Agree	Not Sure	Percent Not Sure	Disagree	Percent Disagree
I feel that conflict resolution skills are important to teach children.	103	99	1	1	0	0
By teaching conflict resolution skills in the classroom, fewer students have been referred for disciplinary actions.	43	41.4	54	51.9	7	6.7
My students are learning how to manage their conflicts constructively and to solve their own problems.	53	50.9	39	37.6	12	11.5
I do not incorporate conflict resolution skills in my classroom because it requires too much time.	69	66.3	2	1.9	33	31.8

Chart 2A.

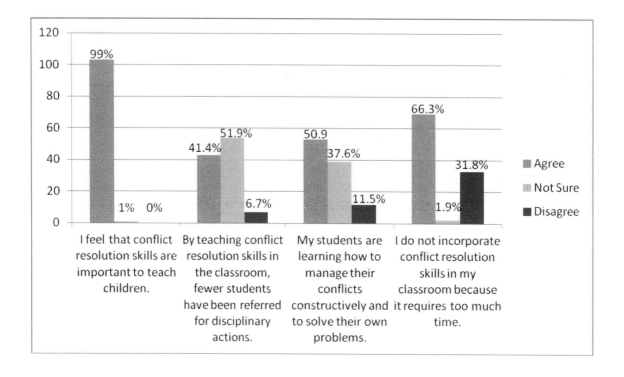

Table 2B.

Statements	Agree	Percent Agree	Not Sure	Percent Not Sure	Disagree	Percent Disagree
I do not incorporate conflict resolution skills in my classroom due to a lack of knowledge in the conflict resolution curriculum.	43	41.3	5	4.8	56	53.9
I do not incorporate conflict resolution skills in my classroom because it is not required at my school.	53	51	9	8.6	42	40.4
I do not incorporate conflict resolution skills in my classroom because it is not needed.	15	14.4	4	3.8	85	81.8
I know some schools that are getting good results by requiring teachers to incorporate conflict resolution skills in the classroom.	51	49	40	38.5	13	12.5

Chart 2B.

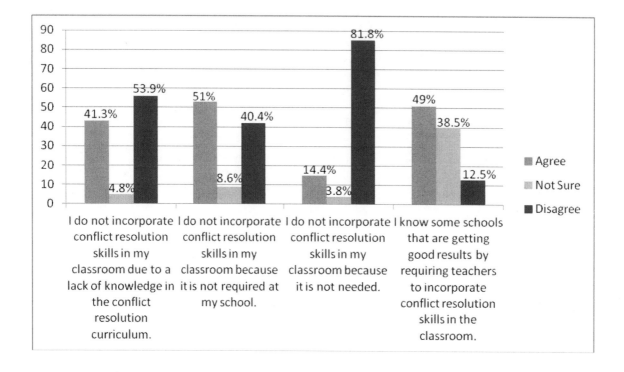

References

Burton, M. (1993). *How teachers make decisions about discipline: The effects of perceptions of similarity or difference teachers and hostile-aggressive students on disciplinary strategy intentions.* [CD-ROM]. Abstract from: Pro-Quest File: Dissertation Abstracts 9413071.

Cheatham, A. (1998). *Directory of school mediation and conflict programs.* Amherst, MA: National Association for Mediation in Education.

Conbere, J. (1994/1995). Peer mediation in a context of systemic change. *The Fourth R*, 54, 5-11.

Conn, E.J. (1989). *Conflict management techniques for kindergarten through fourth grade.* Paper presented at the August 1989 Research Colloquia: Issues in Education, Murray State University, Murray, KY.

Cutrona, C., & Guerin, D. (1994). Confronting conflict peacefully: Peer mediation in schools. *Education Horizons, 72,* 95-104.

DeCecco, J. & Richards, A. (1974). *Growing pains: Uses of school conflict.* New York: Aberdeen Press.

Gentry, D.B., & Benenson, W.A. (1992). School-age peer mediators transfer knowledge and skills to home setting. *Mediation Quarterly, 10*(1), 101-109.

Girard, K. & Koch, S.J. (1996). *Conflict resolution in the schools: A manual for educators.* San Francisco: Jossey-Bass.

Hoover, D.R. (1990). *Relationships among perceptions of principals' conflict management behaviors, levels of conflict, and organizational climate in high schools.* [CD-ROM]. Abstract from: Pro-Quest File: Dissertation Abstracts Item: 9032296.

Johnson, D.W., Johnson, R.T., & Dudley, B. (1992). Effects of peer mediation training on elementary school students. *Mediation Quarterly, 10*(1), 89-99.

Johnson, D.W. & Johnson, R.T. (1996). Reducing school violence through conflict resolution training. *Preventing Violence in Schools, 40,* 11-18.

Johnson, L.W. (1991). *The effects of conflict management training upon the conflict management styles of teachers.*

Joyce, B., Weil, M., & Showers, B. (1992). *Models of teaching.* Boston: Allyn & Bacon.

Koplow, L. (2002). *Creating schools that heal: Real-life solutions.* New York: Teachers College Press.

Kreider, W.J. (1991). *Creating peaceable classrooms in elementary schools.* NIDR Forum, Spring, 5-8.

Lam, J. (1987). *The impact of conflict resolution programs on schools: A review and synthesis of the evidence.* Amherst, Massachusetts: National Association Mediation in Education (NAME).

Lantieri, L. (2003). Waging peace in our schools: The resolving conflict creatively program. In M.J. Elias, H. Arnold, & C.S. Hussey, (Eds.), *Best leadership practices for caring and successful schools* (76-88). Thousand Oaks, CA: Corwin Press.

Leckona, T. (1991). *Educating for character: How our schools can teach respect and responsibility.* New York: Bantom.

McKinney, T.T., Berdiansky, H.A., & Johnson, J.L. (1992). *Peers empowering peers: The action challenge: Peer mediation.* Raleigh, NC: North Carolina State University.

Meek, M. (1992). *The peacekeepers: Teaching tolerance.* (ERIC Document Reproduction Service No. EJ 458727).

Messing, J.K. (1991). *Conflict resolution on the elementary school level. Annual review of conflict knowledge and conflict resolution.* New York: Garland.

Mild, R.E. (1990). *An analysis of conflict management in grades 3-8.* Pittsburgh, PA.

NAME (National Association for Mediation in Education), 1987. *"Project SMART: School Mediators' Alternative Resolution Team."* New York: Victim Services Agency.

Rifkin, J. (1991). An overview of dispute resolution in educational institutions. *Forum, Spring, 1-4.*

Schacht, C.R. (1994). *Development and implementation of a school mediation program.* Greenville, NC: East Carolina University.

Statistical Abstract of the United States, 113th edition, 1993. Washington, DC: *U.S. Government Printing Press.*

Stuart, L.A. (1991). *Conflict resolution using mediation skills in the elementary schools.* Charlottesville, VA: University of Charlottesville.

Trevaskis, D.K. (1994). *Mediation in schools.* ERIC Clearinghouse for Law-Related Education. (ERIC Document Reproduction Service No. ED 378108).

About the Author

Samantha K. Jones-Woodard focuses on addressing the counseling and guidance needs of learners to improve the "whole" student. She is committed to implementing intervention strategies to encourage and facilitate students' improvement in conflict resolution, self-esteem, social skills, motivation, readiness, and academic success. Her professional experiences include counseling, teaching at the early childhood level, teaching at the elementary level, and teaching at the community college level. Her inspiration is helping inspire students to become "thirsty" for the knowledge and skills needed to become productive citizens in society. She aims to help students to be able to reach their academic goals, life goals, and career aspirations.

Samantha K. Jones-Woodard's educational experiences include a Bachelor's Degree in Elementary Education with a specialization in Early Childhood Education, a Master's Degree in Counseling, and a Doctorate Degree in Educational Leadership with a specialization in Teaching and Learning. All of her experiences include promoting a collaborative education model in classroom settings.

12882110R00041

Printed in Great Britain
by Amazon.co.uk, Ltd.,
Marston Gate.